A TRUEBIES GUIDE, PART 2

A TRUEBIES GUIDE, PART 2

ALESIA "TRUE" CORPENING

Copyright © 2020 by J Merrill Publishing, Inc.

All rights reserved. No part of this publication may be reproduced, distributed, or transmitted in any form or by any means, including photocopying, recording, or other electronic or mechanical methods, without the prior written permission of the publisher, except in the case of brief quotations embodied in critical reviews and certain other noncommercial uses permitted by copyright law. For permission requests, write to the publisher, addressed "Attention: Permissions Coordinator," at the address below.

ISBN: 978-1-950719-32-7 (Paperback)
ISBN: 978-1-950719-33-4 (eBook)

Library of Congress Control Number: 2020907955

FIRST printing edition 2019.

J Merrill Publishing, Inc.
434 Hillpine Drive
Columbus, OH 43207

www.JMerrillPublishingInc.com

Blessed is the man who perseveres during trials, - James 1:12

Sometimes I wish raising you was as simple as black and white.

I wish the hues were signs of what to do next.

There's no rule book or how-to manual, so with you, I do my best.

To my children, you are a slave to no one, not even your own mind.

No one told me that my experience with you would unleash a journey like this.

Filled with twist and turns,

I'm far from perfect, but I'll always do my best to lead by example and only pray that all this soaks in your mental.

Be kind, but always be aware.

Fear is only an emotional reaction.

You don't know what you don't know; always be teachable, never foolish.

Pride is a foolish man's best friend; hang it on your door before you leave home.

I remember Amari came home and read a poem that said:

Hey Black Child
Do you know who you are
Who you really are
Do you know you can be

What you want to be
If you try to be
What you can be

And until there's no breath in me, this will define me.

I must show you the tools to help you define who you are, where you are going, and what life is about.

Believe in perfect timing - kind of like the way Sincere repeatedly asked the same question 10 times for reassurance - You are a slave to no one, so you'll have to master perfect timing.

Understand that until there's no life in me, I'll provide you with the fundamentals, and that won't always look so gentle.

Sometimes, I'll yell. Sometimes, I'll cry but know that.

I am a slave to no one, not even my own mind. So, until you're sitting on the top of the city gazing at the skyline, I'll be a slave to no one and always show up on time.

A wise man can learn more from a foolish question than a fool can learn from a wise answer. - **Bruce Lee**

CONTENTS

Introduction ... ix

LESSON I
1. Silence the noise so you can find yourself. ... 3
2. Action Steps ... 5
3. S.W.O.T ... 9

LESSON II
4. Know where your finish line is ... 13
5. Action Steps ... 15
6. G.R.O.W.T.H ... 17
7. Building Consensus ... 19
8. Action Steps ... 21

LESSON III
9. Know your shit ... 25
10. Action Steps ... 29

LESSON IV
11. Your word is bond ... 35
12. Action Steps ... 37

LESSON V
13. If you don't know how, you won't know when ... 41
14. Action Steps ... 43

LESSON VI
15. Cash or credit? ... 49
16. Action Steps ... 51

LESSON VII

17. Don't stay in the water, if it's over your head; you'll drown 55
18. Action Steps 57

LESSON VIII

19. You have bragging rights. You're somebody now! 61
20. Action Steps 63

LESSON IX

21. Blessed is the man who perseveres during trials 69

LESSON X
BONUS CONTENT

22. Process & Systems 73
23. Vendors List 77
24. Marketing Tools 81

Also by Alesia "True" Corpening 83

Introduction

> *Life is simply a series of moments while our emotions are how we respond to these moments. The sooner we learn to master our emotions, the sooner we accept our series.*

Originally, I thought I'd give you all these tools I used to accomplish things and call it a how-to-guide. I later realized the tools don't matter without the journey. The journey is what makes us and keeps us whole. The journey is the true transformation.

I have a million and one things on my "Get my shit together" to-do list, and the one question that repeats over and over is where do I start?

As each day passes, I realize that I accomplish a little day by day, but that never seems to be enough.

I'm unsure if I've spent too much time scrolling on social media, teaching others, or too much time planning the perfect direction to move in. But, the burden of feeling stagnant is being dumped from my shoulders right now.

INTRODUCTION

Besides, I've been studying the game diligently through experience for the last five years. So there's been a lot of trial and error to get to this point. I've incorporated over 20 companies and worked with professionals all over the world.

The goal of this book is to be completely transparent in my journey and to share with you the tools I use to overcome daily adversities as a black mother and entrepreneur in 2020 America.

Throughout this book, you'll find some adversities I've faced in my personal life, how they impacted my business world, and what tools I put in place to overcome them. Most of this book is short stories, how-tos, and worksheets. The only promise I'm making is that if you don't implement anything, you won't get anywhere. I don't have all the answers, and I won't pretend to. There are thousands of self-help books, gurus, Google, Facebook, TedTalk, YouTube, and the list goes on; pick one that relates to you and start. Most of the questions you may have around growing your brand on social media will be found in "A Truebies Guide Pt.1" (which you can download for FREE on our website thetruecreatives.com)

Many of you reading were introduced through social media, some experience we've had together, or you were recommended to read this book by a friend.

Either way, I'm going to take a moment to get acquainted before I dive in.

I'm True, born and raised in Cleveland, Ohio. The stories I'm about to share come from a space of passion, experience, and development. To understand where I am, you must understand where I've been.

 Poverty - the state of being inferior in quality or insufficient in amount.

I can't teach what I don't know.

I'm here to show you that living in poverty is a mindset, not a physical thing.

INTRODUCTION

Every answer we need is out there. There's always potential to change your current situation by walking through a new door. And when that door is locked, we must find the key or knock it down.

Our ducks should have been in a row a long time ago. We're late to the party, and we're not okay. I never thought in 2020, I'd be fighting for the same liberty that my ancestors fought for. But I am, we are, and the only way to win that fight is to educate ourselves, our family, our children, and our neighbors.

We must build a sustainable community amongst ourselves and understand that we're not here just to get through. We have the liberty to live how we want to live.

No one is forcing us to *accept* the bare minimum.

It's up to us as individuals to go for what we want and build social, emotional, and financial freedom no matter what the roadblocks look like.

Some say money isn't everything. However, money pays for everything we desire and require. Therefore, I say, if we want more time with our family, or to teach ourselves beyond the resources given to us, we must earn a sustainable amount of currency of some kind, a.k.a. Assets.

My mother purchased a little blue book with unicorns on it for me when I was 13 years old. It reads, "To: Alesia, this will help you to get a lot of things & thoughts off of your mind. Talk or write to yourself... it helps. Love you, Mommy.'

INTRODUCTION

> To: Alesia
> This will help you to get alot of things & thoughts off of your mind. Talk or write to yourself....
> It helps
> Love you
> Mommy.

It was given to me shortly after my grandmother's boyfriend had molested me. The experience made me shut down. Although I wasn't penetrated, I felt my innocence was ripped from me in that moment. So, speaking about how I feel or what I want is something I lost sight of early on. That book was the first place I began manifesting the life I want.

INTRODUCTION

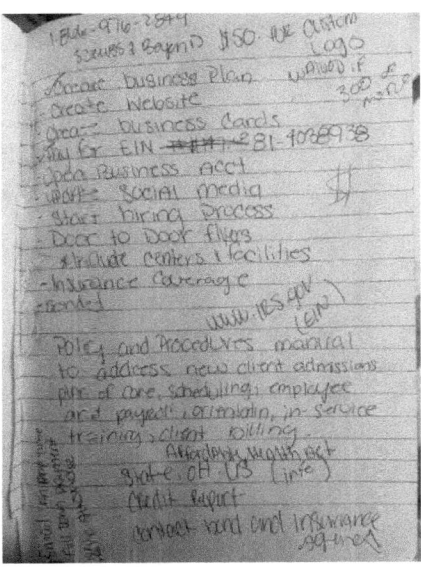

At 16, when I became an STNA. I had no understanding that I'd be signing up to put a cap on my pay.

When I decided to become an entrepreneur, I had no idea of the journey I was about to experience. I most certainly did not expect to be writing this book and adding 'published author' to my list of accomplishments. It wasn't until I realized the true power of manifestation that I understood the experiences of the world happens for us and not to us.

That understanding came from a reading I had on August 7, 2018.

INTRODUCTION

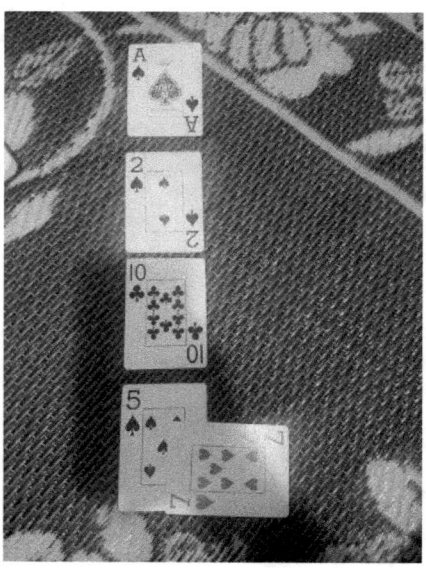

My cards fell as pictured above. The reading was given for free at Ifawuyi.com. My question was, will the decisions I'm making have a positive impact on my children's future? Her response was: "IFA says yes, the decisions that you are making now will have a positive effect on your children in the future. It is a positive reading. You will have good fortune. Just be patient, and don't be spiteful. I used playing cards to get clarity for the rest of the reading. The cards fell all black and more spades, which means this reading involves your career.

Ace of Spades: It is something that you are concealing or keeping a secret about your finances and yourself.

2 of Spades: This deals with communication with yourself and others. You need to keep harmony and stay away from wars or disputes.

10 of Clubs: This is dealing with the heart; you are curious and sometimes put on a show.

5 of Clubs: Is the foundation here. It is the crossroads, you feel trapped uncertain, and you have a fear of change.

INTRODUCTION

7 of hearts: This card was a double card. It was not intended to be pulled. It goes with the crossroads and the foundation. You are being challenged to live the truth.

Topic: Secrets
Not to Do: Get into disputes
Need to be: Clever and be light-hearted
Results: If you challenge yourself to live the truth, you won't feel trapped and be fearful of change."

I began a process called "The 4 Step Cure" with that same priestess shortly after this reading. The goal was and continues to be, to learn myself, stay grounded, and manifest the life I want.

When I started True Creatives, it was solely off the idea of not interning for someone else's company. I knew my goal was to own a business that makes a profit. I never expected to have seven clients within three months of being in business.

Well, with supply comes demand. I opened my doors to a personal assistant to handle client accounts and some communications. After an hour's phone interview, which was only supposed to be 15 minutes, Ms.E joined my team. In short, Ms.E is a local baker and now friend here in Cleveland, Ohio, and she makes these amazing "Glory Loaves."

I had no idea that being a part of TCM would open the doors of opportunity when it comes to learning new technology to implement in her business. Ms.E went on a hell of a journey with me from working from home to upgrading into an office space, gaining clients, and losing them, and so much more.

Eventually, I had to make a hard decision and end our business endeavors as being an assistant. As organized and as great as she is in handling business, I knew I was holding her back from her capabilities during my time of growth and lesson building.

"HELLO, MA'AM!" Loudly came from the other end of the phone after hitting the green button. I had to look at the phone due to the excitement I heard. Ms.E continued, "Um, we need to update my

INTRODUCTION

website for orders and my landing page. Did you see the mail I sent out? What about a discount code? Can I text people? I had over 20 orders in 24 hours. I need to contact all of these people and get ship..."

I quickly stopped her there. "Well, congratulations! However, you are not calling all those people one by one, Ericka! Seriously it's time we update your systems to meet your demand."

Fast forward, Ms.E's Glory Loaves can be purchased worldwide online at Gloryloaves.com (website and systems courtesy of me). The best part of that is she understands "Most" of the systems behind her company. She understands the importance of continually connecting with her audience no matter where they are in the buying process and what techniques to implement based on that information. Because Ms.E has made over $20,000 and counting and has managed to not only understand but implement marketing communication techniques without my overseeing, I am confident and proud to hand her the title of my biggest success story to date. My goal is to add your company to the list of success stories.

The thing I love most about helping others build their brand is that I express things that most people won't tell you.

Your first lesson is as follows:

- Overcome all adversities by studying them and taking them head-on
- Have an exit strategy
- Learn yourself
- Understand why you need to communicate with your audience
- Make hard decisions FAST
- Audit everything including yourself
- Give yourself credit when it's due
- Fail Forward
- Entrepreneurship isn't easy, and it isn't for the weak. Yet it's achievable!

LESSON I

Silence the noise so you can find yourself.

The loud click, followed by the vibration of the clippers, felt pleasant on my hands. It was so calming at that moment. As I stare in the mirror, my eyes start to gloss. I feel lost in this moment.

As my hair hits the floor, I start to feel a sense of relief. I inhaled deeply before brawling about every aspect of my life in combination with this horrible ass haircut I gave myself — literally a Brittany moment, Truebies. At that moment, I realized I had control of my outcome. I took this moment of weakness and figured out who I am, what I truly want, how I want to spend my life, should I leave my boyfriend, and every other question your average 23-year-old wants to know.

Truebs — I was depressed, and it showed. The best thing I did at this time was to write out my ideas on paper.

Action Steps

A man with a plan gets further. Place a goal you want to tackle in the number spaces. In the letter slots, add one thing you must do to accomplish that goal (action step). Add more letters if necessary. Upon completion, we'll add those steps to your to-do list, set reminders and deadlines in your personal calendar to help keep you consistent. This does not have to be followed in chronological order; the goal is to simply get started taking action.

Example.

I. Build Engagement with a core audience
a. Host monthly events that teach my techniques
- Create a curriculum
- Find A location to host
- Create a price

b. Post daily to all social platforms
- Create content that fits the focus list & teaches my audience
- Plan content one month in advance
- Follow calendar

ALESIA "TRUE" CORPENING

I.

A.

B.

C.

II.

A.

B.

C.

III.

A.

B.

C.

IV.

A.

B.

C.

V.

A.

B.

C.

"If I don't know what I am, I must know what I'm not "

S.W.O.T

S.W.O.T - A 4-step analysis that helps you identify your strengths, weaknesses, opportunities, and threats. The goal is to understand how to prepare you and your business and what tools you'll need to implement to be successful.

Think about your strengths and weaknesses, both personal and business. Now it's time to get them on paper to help secure your brand image.

Answer the questions as honestly as you can. If you want to share your response, you can email them to me at atruebiesguide@gmail.com.

What does your product/service offer?
How important is the offer to your consumers?
Are your consumers intrigued by your service/product?
What are the key features of your product/services?
What are the benefits?
Who is the consumer?
What do they need?
What is the value of your service/product to them?
What is your competition offering?

Do they offer discounts? How Much? How Often?
What are their special offers?
How will you promote your product/services outside of using our services?
Do you have proof or reassurance of your service benefits?
Do you have systems and processes in place?
What are your strengths? (attributes and resources that leads to success)
What are your weaknesses? (Internal attributes and resources that works against your success)
What opportunities do you have? (external factors to capitalize and use to advance)
What threats are present? (External or internal factors that could jeopardize success)
Specify your goals.
What do you do better than anyone else?
What advantages do you have?
Where do you need improvement?
What market trends could increase sales?
Where do competitors have market advantages?

LESSON II

Know where your finish line is

I hit the ground running — absolutely no clue where I was running to. I just knew I could learn whatever I needed about starting a business, and I had five years of experience as an STNA to back up whatever idea I came up with.

September 2016, Sincere Private Homecare LLC was born. When that didn't work out how I planned, mainly from a combination of no money and no marketing experience, I went back to work.

My definition of marketing at that time was creating a Facebook page, telling all my family and friends, and printing business cards and flyers.

That's where my 5x5 rule was born. Every day I opened my eyes, I'd go to my neighborhood and post my flyers in every business that would allow me to. The rule is — Go to, at least, 5 places per week. Every place you go, you should leave at least 5 business cards or promotional items in each location and REPEAT.

Four businesses, hell of failures and wins, a life coach, every eBook, coaching call, or webinar you can think of, and a communications trade later —

ALESIA "TRUE" CORPENING

The biggest lesson I've learned here was to start from the end and work backward.

Action Steps

Ask yourself

What is your end goal for your business or brand?

How much money do you want to make per year? How much would you have to make per day to reach that goal?

Use this formula to calculate how much you need to make per day before you can replace your day job.

Yearly Money Goal ÷ 12 (Amount of months) = Monthly Money Goal

Monthly Money Goal ÷ 4 (Amount of weeks in a month) = Weekly Money Goal

Weekly money Goal ÷ 7 (Amount of days in a week) = Daily money Goal

Example: I want to replace my day job with a business. I currently make 30,000 per year.

30,000 ÷ 12 = 2,500

2,500 ÷ 4 = 625

ALESIA "TRUE" CORPENING

625 ÷ 7 = 89.28 (Round Up)

Daily Money Goal = $90.00

G.R.O.W.T.H

I worked with a lady once, and she gave me an additional tool called the G.R.O.W. tool. Here we're going to call it G.R.O.W.T.H because I've added a few letters.

Use this to help define where you are and where you're going. The dope part about this tool is that it helps you audit yourself or your situation in a realistic way. It's also universal. I use this tool in business and personal relationships to help build consensus. My partner and I stopped pursuing a relationship after using this tool; don't let that scare you, though. It's a good thing.

What we and by we, I mean HE, realized after sitting for a few hours and completing this assignment together, was that what I wanted and expected, he wasn't ready for. He never said he didn't want it. The tool just helped him realize we lacked communication and understanding, which in return would affect all the things that I wanted. So, we decided that separating was the best way forward. We'll revisit the rest of this later. Let's discuss building consensus. Remember, this tool is designed to evaluate one's self or to be used as a conversation forum when communicating with someone else.

Building Consensus

Consensus - An agreement

Building Consensus - Problem-solving and decision making that has inclusiveness

What it isn't

1. A unanimous vote
2. Everyone getting what they want
3. Being Completely satisfied with the outcome
4. The "right "option

What it is

1. Everyone understands the decision & why its best
2. Everyone can live with it

What it takes

1. Time
2. Active participation of everyone involved

3. Skills in communication
4. Listening
5. Conflict resolution & facilitation (making a process or action easier)
6. Creative thinking
7. Being open-minded

Action Steps

G.R.O.W.T.H - Goals, Reality, Options, Wayforward, Transcendence, Harmony

What are your goals?

What's the reality of your goals?

What options do you have to reach your goals?

Out of the options you chose, which best fits as a way to move forward?

What are you willing to experience, accept, or do beyond normal activities to reach those goals?

How will your decision co-exist with your end goal?

LESSON III

Know your shit

No matter how you want to word it, the objective is to stay ready — Okay, Truebies, now let's break down some systems.

Cashflow: Your cash flow is the amount of debt you have and the amount of income you have, better known as assets (things that make you money) and liabilities (things you spend money on). In this case, we'll be either **A**. Projecting your cash flow or **B**. Measuring your previous cash flow before doing **A.**

My goal is to help you understand the current or projected cash flow of your business. This activity will help you

- Understand your cash flow
- Learn to project, plan, and prepare for your cash flow

Your cash flow helps you:

- Understand the use of your finances (money)
- Prepare for capital injection (how much money you invest in your company)
- Plan for the next three years of business

- Define your need versus your spend

It's critical to understand where your money comes from and where it goes in your business.

When thinking about the following positions of a company, keep in mind where you currently are and where you're headed. If you're a new entrepreneur, you may be wearing all these hats. Others may have delegated some of these positions to digital systems or hired employees or contractors. Review the information below, answer the questions, then create a spreadsheet with detailed categories listing expenses, debt, income, loans, and investments.

We're going to plan for the next three months, six months, 12 months, and 3 years of business.

The goal is to define the needs of your specific business, and project the cost and profit of it.

Positions of a company:

Business Development - Market research; where is your company position in the market

Visionary/CEO - thinks outside the box, the head of the company usually the owner founder or co-founder

Operations - Builds systems that carry a client from point A to point B and communicates with process management to ensure quality

Finance - Bookkeeping, document all cash flow including but not limited to expenses, profits, net (income after all deductions), and gross (income before any deductions) income.

Expansion - the location of the company, where it will grow to, areas it will service

Marketing - Builds strategies to connect with your target audience to increase sales

Legal - Compliance and permits including but not limited to contracts

Information - Research, current trends, changes in the market

Product Development - Makes improvements to products based upon customer feedback and market trends

Sales - Closes deals, customer relationship management, promotes the business to gain a profit

The strategy is to allow your systems to drive your business.

Action Steps

How well is my system?

Who's driving my system?

How much does it cost to run and operate each part of my system?

What fees do I pay to run my company?

How much does my company make per month?

How much did my company make in the last 12 months?

How much do I want my company to make in the next 3, 6, 12 months? What about 3 years?

Who is my target audience?

Where will my next sale come from?

How will I get it?

How will I meet my monthly finance goals?

What equipment expenses do I have?

How much credit do I have?

How much money do I owe?

How much money will I invest?

Remember:

- Products and personality are essential, but systems are critical to retaining sales
- Think BIG
- Celebrate your accomplishments but not for long, you need to focus on sales
- Time how long you work in your business and on your business
- What actions will bring you the highest returns in investments?
- What do you have to leverage?
- List all categories of expenses
- Gross profit
- Net profit
- Revenue (Price & Quantity)
- Need vs. Spend
- Service vs. products (Income, Debt, Projections)
- Return on Investment
- Ability to repay a loan, if applicable

* Working in your business is the time you spend providing a service or product.

* Working on your business is the time you spend developing your company and improving your systems and processes.

LESSON IV

Your word is bond

When we're speaking of credit, character means how you pay back what you borrow. But when we're talking about business, character is how your consumer perceives you. My goal is to help you understand your unique selling proposition (USP) or what makes you different, your character. This activity will help you:

- Understand what you want your brand to tell the world
- Learn to connect with your audience
- Learn storytelling techniques

Your brand story helps define the voice of your brand. It's up to you to decide what story you want to tell to connect your product or service with your audience.

If I am not for myself, who will be for me?

If I am for myself alone, what am I?

If not now, when?

Create urgency for action through storytelling.

ALESIA "TRUE" CORPENING

You'll need to know this now so you can understand building calls to action later.

Action Steps

There's three (3) type of stories to tell

- Story of self (USP- Answers why you do what you do)
- Story of us (connects what you do with your consumer)
- Story of now (Creates a sense of urgency)

Stories are a powerful way to receive new clients.

The goal is to connect the head with the heart through storytelling.

After 4-7 encounters, the client already has thoughts of purchasing. The desire is already there because you're solving a problem they have.

The strategy is to allow the motivation of the story to lead to action.

When you're looking for a story to tell, understand that challenges and hope inspire stories, the objective is to allow the public narrative to have a clear understanding of your story.

When telling a story to your audience:

Stick to one moment, then grow into the bigger picture. Only pick stories you're comfortable with telling and remember to include a challenge, a choice, and an outcome.

Remember:

- When you arrived at the challenge, did you face it or quit?
- What choice did you make? Describe it.
- What was the outcome?

The choice around the challenge gives hope to the audience; providing hope is what leads to sales.

Double-check:

- Avoid telling stories in chronological order or resume form
- Pick a specific experience to tell a story about
- Pick choice points - What were you called for today? Why are you telling this specific story? Deciding this will help you know what the bigger picture is.
- Remember that you're the essential character- tell the story through your eyes
- Be vivid and specific, use descriptive words and focus on 1-2 points
- Describe the challenge in the story
- Use a story that illustrates your values
- Use universal emotions (Sad, Happy, Joyful, Confused, Uneasy)

LESSON V

If you don't know how, you won't know when

Systems are the how of your business. How do I book an appointment? How do I pay you? How do I communicate with you? You want your systems to flow as easily as possible because they ultimately create the customers' experience and determine whether they will return or not.

My goal is to help you learn the basic systems your business needs. This activity will help you

- Check your system for any missing components
- Learn to build your system

Your basic systems should include

- Appointment Booking
- Customer Feedback
- Payment Processor
- Email communications
- SMS communications
- Customer relationship management
- Website/ e-commerce store

Each part of your system will use a different platform. Some will share a platform. The goal is to find one system that manages all aspects of your business. Today, we're covering the basic systems that can grow with you and cuts overhead costs for the first 3 years of growth.

Action Steps

Explore each application listed below to help improve or create your systems. These are ones that I currently use or started out using.

Appointment Booking - Square Appointments allows for easy customer management and appointment booking

Acuity

Apointy

Setmore

Customer Feedback - Know what your customers think of your service or product by receiving feedback through forms and polls—using Google forms. Use the link below to set up a G-Suite account.

Slick text

Email

https://gsuite.Google.com/

Payment Processor - Accept payments from all major credit and debit cards by setting up your services inside of Square. Transfer payments directly to your bank account or receive a debit card via Square.

https://squareup.com/us/en

https://www.paypal.com/us/webapps/mpp/home-merchant

https://stripe.com/

Email communications - Communicate with your audience through email

https://mailchimp.com/

https://www.constantcontact.com/

SMS communications - Communicate with your audience through text message

https://www.slicktext.com/

Customer relationship management - Manage your customer accounts, send surveys, spreadsheets, and more. Try their free version if you're just getting started

https://gsuite.Google.com/

https://www.hubspot.com/

Website/e-commerce

https://www.ecwid.com/

https://www.shopify.com/

https://www.squarespace.com/

https://www.weebly.com/

The strategy is to allow your systems to drive your business.

Ask yourself:

How will my customer contact me?
How will they pay me?

How often will they pay me?
How will I communicate with my potential or previous customers?

Remember:

- Products and personality are essential, but systems are critical to retaining sales
- Quality AND Convenience

LESSON VI

Cash or credit?

As a business owner, you want to establish a line of credit for business growth needs. You want to know your credit score, and you want to check your credit report at least once per year. My goal is to walk you through the basic steps of knowing your status. This activity will help you

- Get a free copy of your credit report
- Understand what to look for on your credit report
- Check your report for errors

Your credit report is a record of your bill-paying history, public information, and inquiries by creditors.

Landlords, employers, and lenders use credit reports. Having credit available to you is a great way to use OPM (other people's money) to make investments and triple your profits.

Action Steps

Get a free copy of your credit report. Check your credit every 12 months through the ONLY federally authorized source for free credit reports. Although there are hundreds of credit agencies, most report the largest three (3) agencies are Transunion, Equifax, and Experian. All three reports may be different because they are competitors and do not share information:

Visit **AnnualCreditReport.com or Call 877.322.8228** to get a copy of your credit report for free.

Review your credit report for errors:

Be sure to fix any errors you find and check for identity theft.

Check for:

- Accounts that aren't yours
- Wrong account status ("default," "delinquency," wrong dates of delinquency, listed late, incorrect balances, listed more than once)
- Ensure that each account is only open by one creditor

Double-check:

- Your name (including spelling)
- SSN
- Telephone number
- Current address
- Are previous addresses listed correctly?
- Employment history correct
- Is the public records section correct?
- Credit account/trade account- are they yours? Are the accounts that are open supposed to be open?
- Is the status of each account's description correct?
- Are you an authorized user, co-signer, or joint owner? Is this correct?
- Are your paid or settled consumer accounts closed by the consumer?

I purchased a great course at https://diycreditbook.com/, which has easy ready to go templates to send to the credit bureaus to dispute any errors you may find.

You may also want to consider opening an account with Self, a loan builder site used to help build your credit score.

https://self.inc/refer/18287603

LESSON VII

Don't stay in the water, if it's over your head; you'll drown

I remember telling my mother I wanted to sell cookies at school. The idea came from my best friend, Jasmine — we haven't talked in years, but she'll forever hold the title.

Jas loved to bake. She would bake all these fancy desserts and make them look like burgers and other items. She's very creative.

We'd stand on her porch and promote her bake sale to the neighborhood so she could make money.

(SN: I can't mention Jasmine without mentioning Briana. They literally helped shape the woman I am today early on!)

Okay, back on track. I was in elementary at the time, and I knew that I could do that same thing without offending my friend because we went to different schools. The cookies sold because (1) the recipe came from my best friend who could bake her ass off, and (2) I can sell salt to a slug thanks to my dad.

Fast forward to high school; I had an entire locker filled with snacks — the good ones, Frooties, Hot chips, Juice, you name it.

Then it was Johnny Lee's. I paired up with my cousin to cook out my mom's kitchen, which leveled up to a bar slot in a local bar called Jolly's Place.

When that ended, I went on to Alesia Eat's — still cooking out the kitchen to make ends meet.

We already discussed SPH LLC. I later became a certified lash technician and started Goddess Lash Company LLC. Lastly is my baby, and the reason you're reading this right now True Creatives Media and Management LLC.

The two things each of these ventures have in common is my passion for making it work and my reality to know when it's not.

Yes, our business is our baby. However, please don't get so attached that you can't determine when it's time to exit. Your growth plan must be feasible for you! The good thing is your LLC never dies, so you can always pick up where you left off.

Action Steps

Ask yourself

Am I willing to sell my business? If so, for how much and after how long?

Is my business capable of withstanding an economic hardship?

What is the projected life span of my business?

LESSON VIII

You have bragging rights. You're somebody now!

I walked through the hotel lobby with my heart pounding and my hands sweating while gripping my business cards with my dominant hand.

As I approached the ballroom, I heard music and laughter. Moving closer, there were men in suits on the dance floor with their whiskey in hand.

In the far back was a group of people speaking, smiling, and ordering food.

I was so damn nervous walking to the table seemed like forever.

I started to doubt myself, so I sat in a booth alone and contemplated turning around and going back home to my comfort zone!

"Hell no, you didn't go through all of this to not go network. Get out your head and go do your thing. You'll be okay. Just say hi. Don't worry about anything else. Now go, damn" was the pep talk I gave myself before lifting a finger or moving a foot.

"Hi, I'm Katrice. What's your name?" The host of business card swap night and creator of Network Notions had just broken my networking virginity.

We spoke for a while. Then she encouraged me to mingle.

I again sat in a little corner, "HELLO MA'AM! I'm Ms.E, author, and creator of Ms.E's Glory Loaves, and this is my accountability partner —" Yes, the same Ms.E I spoke of earlier. You see how the universe always aligns you with the right people and things.

Fast forward an untraceable amount of networking events later. There's not a person I meet that I don't network with. Except for people with bad energy, ugh, perfect time to practice social distancing, right?

I mentioned networking because it's a critical part of growing your business. Remove the fear of promoting or telling people about your business. You should always look for an opportunity to present your services or product.

Action Steps

ABC - Always Be Closing

There's always an opportunity to make a sale, create a list of 10 people that need your service or product, and contact them.

1.

2.

3.

4.

5.

6.

7.

8.

9.

10.

The 5 P's - People, Place, Product, Promotion, Price

Place Product – putting your most valuable products in the right place at the right time.

Ask yourself, where can you distribute your product or service to increase sales?

1. Guest Blogs
2. Influencers
3. TikTok
4. Twitter
5. Instagram
6. Facebook
7. Pinterest
8. Etsy
9. Other Businesses

Promotion & Price – Understanding what's being offered and how to plan for a successful product offering

Create promo sales in advance and save random sales and promotion for trends, for example doing a 19% off sale during COVID-19.

When determining a price for your product, consider the market price (what everyone is selling it for) for that item or service, rate the value of that service and product to the end consumer on a scale from 1-10. Using this information and information from above, choose a price point that allows for a profit.

Remember

1. Prices must cover cost and profits
2. Lower cost means lower prices
3. Audit your price every six months for cost, demand, supply, profit goals, and competition
4. No prices mean No Sales

I want to take a second to highlight number 3 - If the following happens, audit your prices.

- New product release
- An economic recession
- Your service or product increases someone's income
- You changed your sales strategy
- You create a new business
- Your cost changes

Here's a formula you can use: Materials + Labor + Overhead = Cost + Desired Profit = Sale Price

Example. 40.00+20.00+60.00 = 120.00 + 45 = $165.00

PEOPLE - YOUR BUSINESS LIVES AND THRIVES BECAUSE OF PEOPLE! Treat people with integrity, follow your gut, be authentic, and connect with genuine people.

LESSON IX

Blessed is the man who perseveres during trials

The most significant lesson trials have taught me are to provide for myself, be intentional, and assertive even when you don't know the how or understand the why! We can't lean on or depend on anyone to mold us into what we want to be or to do the work for us.

Ask yourself, why are you doing what you're doing, and how much more can you do. This will matter later.

I share my journey with the people who feel like no one understands them because that's me. I'm usually talking to myself more than I'm talking to anyone else in my messages, the message is generally for me, and I'm sharing it with the world. Well, my Truebies.

What is that? — A Truebie is someone true to themself. They know where they are and where they want to be. They don't allow their circumstances to define them. They just attack shit and keep growing.

Investing in my mind was one of the best decisions I've ever made. I can now share that knowledge with my Truebies in many forms.

Humans are like plants and sharks. We only grow as large as our environment. If we stay in a small closed environment, we'll grow, but not to our fullest potential.

ALESIA "TRUE" CORPENING

These are tools and information that have worked for clients and me. I motivate you to understand your power and understand that with the right tools and mindset, everything is possible.

- True

LESSON X
BONUS CONTENT

Process & Systems

Goal: To create an exquisite digital experience for customers that helps grow your brand/business

System: (What System do you use to Correct Spelling & Grammar?) Grammarly www.Grammarly.com

How a potential customer finds us AKA Leads

Systems - HotCards, Office Max, MailChimp, Instagram, Facebook,

Business Cards, Banners, Key Chains, QR Codes, Social Media Promotion, A-B-C-List Advertisement, Email List, SMS, Flyers

- Advertising
- Promotion
- Influencer promotion
- Word of mouth
- 5 x 5

How we find a potential customer (Leads)

Facebook & Instagram, Personal Contacts, Eventbrite, TicketBudbud

What is your end goal? - What brands do you want to work with? What type of clients do you want to service? How much money do you want to make? Use one-three words

- Vendor events
- Networking events
- Social media categorized post
- Word of mouth

How we follow up with leads -

- Email - MailChimp
- Phone call / Webinar / Video Conference - Zoom, Google Voice (Pre-Recorded Calls)
- SMS - Slick Text

How we decide what the customer needs -

- Client Intake - Google Forms / Consultation
- Client Research - Remote, Web, Previous History, Social Media, MSRP
- Market Research
- Strategy - Based on collected information and target client profile

How the customer tells us what they need

- Client Intake - Google forms

How we close a sale

- Invoice - Square
- Contracts - Google Docs / AdobeSign
- NDA - AdobeSign

How we communicate with the client during & after the sale

- Brand Development Training - Google Classroom
- Email - Business Email
- Zoom conference
- Google Classroom
- SMS
- How to videos - Google Classroom
- Monthly conference calls - Zoom

How we perform the services

- Time frame - Each Service is a different time frame
- Needed information - Google Classroom Orientation Folder - Each Service has a user-friendly how-to guide
- Systems needed - Understand all systems, so you know what to apply - study materials in Google classroom
- Strategy - Monthly meetings based on analytics

How we retain customers -

- Follow-through - meet deadlines
- Follow up - respond to needs
- Connect - understand needs
- Provide - give them what they need and some of what they want
- Add value - go the extra mile

How we add value to potential customers -

- Tips on why they should grow
- Lead by example

How we add value to current customers -

- Follow-through
- Identify their needs

How we turn leads into customers -

- Follow up one week after initial conversation/interaction and every 3-5 days after that
- Add value whether they purchase now or later
- Offer incentives - coupons and discount codes through Square
- Stay committed and consistent - automate follow-ups
- Take care of current customers - get feedback through JotForm or Google forms
- Referral program - use Google forms or Slick text for referrals
- Automate instant coupons when they sign up for emails & SMS - Slick text @ Mailchimp

Vendors List

Cosmetics

Misenlashes

Cosmeticindex

Imakelipstick.com

Dreamline Beauty

CLOTHING

Bourling

LAshowroom

Pioneerapparel.com (allows for ordering smaller quantities)

CHILDREN'S CLOTHING

Kiskissing.com

Wholesalechildrenclothing.com

Honeydewusa.com

Poutinpink.com

Plus Size Clothing

Zenobiafashion.com

Xtaren.com

Book Printing

Create Space - KDP = Amazon.com

Publishingxpress

48hrbooks - 48hourbooks.com

Pendit

Prettyprinting.com

Book Publishers

Pagepublishing

Fire Brand publishing

J Merrill Publishing (www.JMPub.us)

T-Shirts

Printful.com

24hour tee

Jiffyshirts

Tscapparel

Alphabroder

Losangelesapparel.net

Yazbekusa.com

@mr.officals.llc on Instagram

DropShipping (you don't hold inventory or control shipping)

Oberlo (You'll need a Shopify account)

Modaclyst

Printful

Marketing Tools

Packaging

Stickermule.com

Uprinting.com

Nextdayflyers.com

Packlane.com

FLYERS

Primaflyers.com

Printrunner.com

Hotcards.com

STICKERS

Stickeryou.com

Stickermule.com

ALESIA "TRUE" CORPENING

Hot cards.com

PRINTING

Hotcards.com

MOCKUPS

Placeit.net

NETWORKING

Linktree

Popl.co

Also by Alesia "True" Corpening

Book 1

Book 2

Book 3

www.ingramcontent.com/pod-product-compliance
Lightning Source LLC
Chambersburg PA
CBHW052115110526
44592CB00013B/1620